small stones:
a year of moments

small stones:
a year of moments

Fiona Robyn

Published by Lulu

small stones: a year of moments
A Lulu book

Published in 2008 by Lulu.com
ISBN: 978-1-4092-0449-7

Book and cover design: Steve Pawinski
Cover photo: Nadezda Firsova
Drawings: Bodhi Hill

acknowledgements

Gratitude to Esther Morgan, Susan Utting and Nicola Weller for their attention to this manuscript.

Gratitude to the blogging community, especially Sage Cohen, Richard Powell, Dave Bonta, Karen Maezen Miller and the author of whiskey river. Such a lot of good stuff out there, and so many good people.

Gratitude to the readers of *a small stone* over the years, and to those to took the time to write and say thank you. It meant a lot.

Much gratitude and love to Steve, as always.

for Suzuki Shunryu – I hope he'd approve

contents

introduction 1
january 3
february 17
march 31
april 45
may 59
june 73
july 87
august 101
september 115
october 129
november 143
december 157

I love it just because it is a stone, because today and now it appears to me a stone.

Hermann Hesse

Lovely snowflakes, they fall nowhere else!

Zen proverb

The sad thing is that the knowledge of impermanence is often not enough for human beings. We have to hit ourselves over the head.

Natalie Goldberg

introduction

a small stone was born during a long rainy drive home from the seaside. My thoughts turned to the prose journal-style blog I'd been writing for some time. It was starting to feel like a pair of too-tight trousers. I wanted to create a place where I could really indulge my love of language, where every word would count. As the windscreen wipers swished back and forth and the radio played something sweet and misty, I started playing around with names for this new space.

The phrase *a small stone* floated up from the ether. I dismissed it immediately. It was too plain, too ordinary. I wanted my blog to dazzle, to astonish, to be alive. My imagination wouldn't let it go. It took me on a long walk, where my eyes snagged on a smooth pale-blue oval stone. I bent to pick it up and put it in my pocket. I turned it over, felt the weight of it in my hand, skimmed my fingers over its granular surface. I saw the stone months later, sitting quietly on a shelf and releasing memories of the walk into the air like bubbles.

I stopped looking for a glitzier blog title. Instead I decided to look for a *small stone* every day for a year. It's difficult to describe exactly what they are, but I know them when I see them. They might be a snatch of overheard conversation, the sun moving behind a cloud, or my cat jumping on the lawn. They set off a quiet 'ah!' inside me, like a toddler saying 'look!' They are nothing special and something special all at once. As time went on, I got better at remembering to notice the world around me. Not just to notice it but to scrutinise it, engage with it, love it. My eyes, ears, nose, mouth and hands opened up.

One year became three, and it felt like time to choose my favourite stones, polish them up and arrange them into a book. I was interested to find themes in what I'd written over the years. *small stones* often appear when I'm in motion, and so there are lots of roadside flowers and squashed animals. People who've lost their way often stop me in my tracks. The living world is important, forever in flux, and I'm a sucker for the beauty of colour – daffodils socking you in the eye, the orange sky inviting you outside. I like eating too, with three near-identical stones admitting to the apple crumble I'd finished off for breakfast.

This book can be read through from beginning to end as the story of a year, but it will work just as well when opened up at random. To savour each *small stone* properly, try to swish the words around in your mouth for a few moments before you move on to take the clothes out of the washing machine or post that letter. I hope they leave a good taste in your mouth. I hope they wake you up a little. Most of all I hope they inspire you to find your own 'pause' button, and to start noticing your own extraordinary/ordinary *small stones*. They are simply, gloriously, all around us.

january

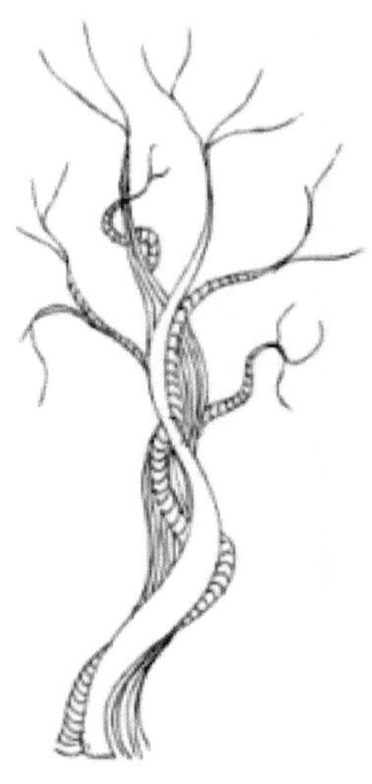

The sun sags in the sky. Half a lemon sits face down in a puddle, scenting the water with citrus. Everything tightens against the cold.

a white cup of golden earl grey breathes a white mist onto the window pane

fat old gentleman pigeon promenades up and down the wall, flicking off specks of snow as he takes in the view

cinamonmmmmm:
hot cross buns with liquefying butter

11 month old Florence says look!
every ten minutes there is something new to fill her up with awe

early morning office:
the pens crackle in their pots with lidded energy

(Year Planner)
the square white days line up: a promise, a threat

(Photos pinned on the office wall)
The vivid reds of mountain ash.
Gnarled rock along a stream.
The stillness of an afternoon.
White birches - yellow leaves.
A spray of pale maples.
Snow-covered rocks
in the Sakauba River.
A brilliant shower of leaves.

driving home, the taste of blood in my mouth

Three days later the sleeping fox is still stretched out on the same patch of grassy verge. The wind makes waves in his pale biscuit fur.

in a Chinese supermarket freezer:
dark purple pig's spleen, creamy honeycomb beef

squeaky piglets truffle in ditches,
roam in gangs across the fields

Small flies emerge from the potted hyacinth one after the other to land on the window-sill next to their squashed brothers. Under the surface, grubs wriggle and wait.

a lost petrol cap leaves a hole like a gaping wound

stencilled fuchsia on a dark green telephone exchange box:
live your life
spray-painted white on a scarlet park bench:
happy?

shyly hiding in the shadow of the hedge: snowdrops!

a splinter of black crosses the blue, keeping its trailing white skirt perfectly straight

only a sprinkling of berries still cling to the bush; pumpkin-coloured, shrunken, holding on tight to their seed

Half-way down this road to nowhere a pair of bus stops have sprung up overnight like mushrooms. Their glass skin is lit up from within.

- white out -
shining headlights into the fog only makes it thicker

(on approaching a small black lump in the road)
expecting death, I find a different kind:
a length of chopped off bough, the leaves still green

the poetry of street signs:
Rose Hill, Blackbird Leys, Iffley

a seam of rubies running underneath the morning –
the voice of a wood-pigeon

one blind open, one blind shut:
the office opposite is winking at me

Crows swagger back and forth across the roof, crying out to each other. A blackbird hops lightly across the car park.

two pots of shocking pink cyclamen flirt with Spring

across the water, behind the rippling bulrushes, three mechanical birds stand with their booms pointing left

At the lights the moustached man in the next car dances his fingers on the steering wheel. His swoops and taps match the music pulsing from my radio. Amber, green. I pull in, park. On stepping out, a bird greets me with a burst of clear-throated song.

sit the vase on the window-sill; light pours into the tulip
blooms, fills the yellow vessels up to the brim

a moment after driving through the white
the rosy smell of bonfires fills the car

A red tractor follows the line of the horizon. Glossy crows perch on stubbled corn. Patches of water help the sky to bear its brilliant blue. Begin again.

february

a crow sits on every tenth fence post
watching for snow clouds

in the cupboard, two fat white Buddhas
each perching on an ancient tin of paint

thwock! - a lump of wet snow chooses this moment to fall
from next door's roof

In the middle of the underpass a television has been beaten to death - twisted metal innards scattered around a pile of shattered glass. Outside a family of ducks nap near the edge of the water with their beaks tucked under their wings as if nothing has happened.

yesterday's snow is grey and blurred against the hot white jabs of "Snowstorm" heather

a robin through binoculars, chest glowing in the darkening afternoon, he dips his body forward and takes black sunflowers seeds into his mouth

city churchyard:
purple crocus,
orange plastic bottle

(Blackbird dance)
He's standing in the middle of a puddle up to his orange ankles. He dips his head beak first into the water and arches upwards. A ripple of shaking starts in his neck and chest and moves outwards to the tips of his wings. The drops fly and glitter.

two blue mooses carved from wood – or is it two blue meece?

cloudy sky at 6am:
the moon a blur, a pale face under ice

An ordinary looking middle-aged woman, she shouts at the top of her voice as she walks along.
For those who want to harm us, a scorn of shame all upon them.
For those who want to harm us, a scorn of shame all upon them.

amongst the graves a plastic bag has tipped onto its side and is spewing human hair out onto the grass

The young man in the tea-shop has *got himself into a mess*; he's been *suicidal for the past three and a half years*. Sometimes it feels like his *head is going to explode*.

a single apple on a leafless tree watches the first flirt of pink deepen into rose until an orange sliver nudges up over the black horizon and leaks light everywhere

The subway guitarist is unshaven, flushed, he smells of the street. Music streams from his tobacco-stained fingers.

an empty bottle of washing up liquid fails to match the yellow of a bunch of sassy daffodils

an old man slumped in the crook of a wall turns back into white plastic bin bags stuffed with empties

in New Look young girls put on different clothes, try to find out who they might be the orange of freshly-split fragrant butternut squash

the moon is so transparent you could slip a thumb-nail under the edge and peel it from the sky

fat sparrow baubles hang on bare branches
every so often they rearrange themselves

pastel clouds heap up on the hills, a cross between marshmallows and candyfloss

in the crease of the dull green valley a clump of dogwood holds up its blood-red branches, a glorious 'V'

three postcards from Iceland:
a building made of ice-bricked domes, light leaking from inside / a blue door with antlers set on deer hides for handles / deer, close-up, yellow clouds rising from their hot mouths

branches flex
leaves shiver
a grey blur darts
(fishlike)
out of sight

a strong gust catches the sheet of plastic – whoop! – the raindrops are flicked into the air: a dog shaking off water, a cloud of dandelion seeds

A crow meows from the roof. Two rabbits wait side by side to cross the road. A blackbird scuttles sideways, intent on pecking something tasty from the tarmac. Who is singing? Phee phee phee… Phee phee phee…

A chip of white moves through the clouds, carrying strangers from somewhere to somewhere else. Closer to home aubergine seeds have pushed their folded white necks out of the dark.

march

daffodil bulbs are warmed into yellow bursts

a pigeon causes a commotion amongst the pink blossoms,
blundering on branches that won't support his weight

a thin worm of green-tinted mint and tea-tree conditioner
piles up in my hand - after rinsing it clean, my scalp zings

out of season: we burn petrol in search of an aubergine

the sudden green of broccoli water as it curls down the silver drain

I sit in a small room all afternoon and swallow yawns. Outside, an unidentified bird twirls his song around him like a streamer.

it's a beautiful tail - jet black, thistle-fluff soft and bushy - but I still don't appreciate it draped across the keyboard as I type

Old poet, he loses his place, ugly-coughs, breaks into snatches of song. He wants to read more poems than time allows. He is so transparent, you can see the back of the hall behind him. He is so solid, when he looked into me and took my hand he squeezed out tears.

the heap of discarded White Lightening bottles huddles closer to the church wall, seeking shelter

(Hoxton Square)
Squirrel. Man drinking cider. Pigeon. A hearse followed by 10 black saloons carrying mourners, heaped with flowers. Sunshine. A toddler called Harry. Pigeon. Squirrel.

He's a middle-aged workman, thick in the waist, with cropped hair and salt-and-pepper stubble. His white T-shirt and jeans are spangled with thousands of rainbow dashes of paint.

through the rain-spattered office windows
empty cars wait patiently for their owners

Reflections of dry-ice clouds drift across the mirror of the windscreen to a back-drop of sunshot blue. The occasional dark bird-shapes dart and swoop.

the houses, fence and car park move so slowly, they fool us into thinking they are static

looking out into the dark
the streetlamps abracadabra the raindrops into gems

moving:
all day we pack our lives into boxes

A Big Issue seller with a lined face is smiling and chatting with three old ladies. Written across the back of his coat in black felt tip is 'working not begging'.

The whole school of girls is lined up in rows, the ones at the back propped up on wooden steps. One of them shakes her hair between shots, wanting to look her best, not thinking about the years ahead when she'll be taking this photo out and studying the faces, looking for clues.

he speaks from his dark and lonely centre:
love brims up in me

The buds on the magnolia trees are pink-tinted and fat. Pull up a chair; wait for them to go bang.

half a drop of blood on a folded white tissue: a girl's woollen hat dropped on a snow hill

a whiff of jasmine tickles the room; the first five-petalled star has opened up

(eclipse)
the pale moon turns ill, slips under a sheet of shadow

She said to me, you are Polish, you should know your place.

a lone man, his detector a pendulum, crosses field after field in search of treasure

(Freudian slip)
She says *intimacy* instead of *impotency*. He says *that's what I'm afraid of.*

gorse sits squat, the ember-blossoms giving off heat and light / lone rapeseed flowers periscope above fields of their short green comrades / forsythia sticks its yellow-encrusted branches into the sky, a finger up at this drab attempt at Spring ten minutes after the kettle boils, tongues of steam still rise from the shining spout

(lit before writing)
extinguished, the burgundy candle kicks out a last burst of cinnamon scent

This morning the sunlight is distilled golden optimism. Even when clouds slip across and shield us, the radio still belts out bright funk-rock. The singer repeats a stolen lyric from 'Come All Ye Faithful'.

the fingernail on Daisy's 5 week old finger's so tiny
I can't think of anything small enough to compare it to

april

look up!
pale orange branches, pale blue sky

a digger tips its scoop: the sand slides out as if from a cupped palm

small voice from the street:
mummy, can you smell farts?

(parked car, early morning)
a full bottle of coca cola, set down on this car roof last night
by someone happy and tired, and then forgotten

The tree is a shapely cloud on a tall, narrow trunk, dripping with white blossoms. Two purple balloons are nestled deep in the tangle of branches, snagged during their break for the sky. They have decided after all that this is a good place to die.

green tea tastes green, and oranges taste orange

the trees cast zig-zag shadows onto the bricks while steam spews from a nearby vent and spreads itself out into nothing

with BALLPOINT PEN written neatly along its length
and a ring of tiny white stars before the 'B'
this pen also deserves our attention

Sunday's giant Easter egg is losing its appeal

a pastel-yellow butterfly mistakes a dandelion for his sister

He has slicked back hair and a sharp suit, and takes a photo of the house before fumbling for a key and letting himself in. The lady who used to live here wore a headscarf which framed her heart-shaped fine-boned face. Her body was a dancer's body, but tired. She always smiled. They carried her into an ambulance and she flew away.

white magnolia petals hang from the branches in beautiful tatters

the birds all cry at once - 'cat! cat! cat!'

Spring cold:
I really miss breathing when I can't

an all-blue billboard
waiting
just off-sky

Despite his bright orange vest he seems too wild-haired to be a Post Office employee. The can of 10 am super-strong lager in his right hand gives him away.

I count them as I pick them up. The fag butts. I count them. That's a quarter of a million since Christmas. I count them as I pick them up.

(chocolate crispie cakes)
I am hungry for more than food today and take five

they stand in the gap between carriages – five big men with red faces, shouting the same words over and over - *ea-SY ea-SY es-SY shaaaad-uuuuuup.....*

(25 Erleigh Road)
The building is unmarked, official looking. Behind the hedge, in the car-park, a young man is sitting alone in his white van and crying his eyes out.

the chequered Snake's head Fritillaries hang their heads and play their silent violins as the evening comes on

like pulling away from a platform:
are the clouds moving, or is it me?

Rather than the open magnolia trees or the scattering of white blossoms on the verges, I remember the word *cunt* drawn into the heavy dust of a traffic sign with a fingertip.

He pulls up his sleeve in the graveyard, where anyone could see him, and waits as his friend hands him something out of sight. His skin is pale, a worm in freshly dug earth.

(early morning in a business park)
old skinny fox, oh where are you going?

She jumps off her bike and knocks the girl over, shouting and kicking her in the head and stomach. Men step in, pull them away from each other. Just further on, a pink pool of cherry blossoms lie under a naked tree. I pick one up, as if it might help. It has no scent. The tissue-thin petals are as soft as the soles of a baby's feet.

like a sudden cloud of pale green, the clean scent of virgin
olive oil fills the carriage

triangle:
power cable
washing line
fading aeroplane-trail

burrow a few Pink Fur Apple potatoes in the soil:
you'll dig up many more when summer comes

(shhhh)
pink and blue sky, whisper of moon, even(bird)song

may

(first harvest)
a pile of peppery rocket squeezed between two slices of buttered granary bread

a blackbird on the roof makes a perfect curve with the line from his tail-feathers to the crown of his head, framing a slice of sky like a cookie-cutter

not music seeping from the floor above
but the fridge's two-tone rhythmic buzz

6.45 am: two crows push their heads into the grass like spears and gobble their breakfast. Behind them the mist is so thick the fields could be on fire.

the water scorched the sweetcorn seedling's leaves
and now they might not make it through the week

an almost-circle of translucent moon pinned on egg-shell blue, above the pink and billowing skirts of clouds

(buttercups)
their shiny petals a shallow dish designed to bounce pure yellow back at the bees

A pale foot-flattened path made by many feet sweeps ahead. An iridescent-blue beetle makes his way from one lush green forest to another.

a string of ducks are out for an early morning waddle,
zig-zagging the road's white lines

the plash plish plash of rain reminds me I'm thirsty

each thick, fermented mouthful of orange and mango juice contains a hundred miniscule bubbles that burst - pap pap pap - on my tongue

Here with his anxious parents and his quiet girlfriend, he sits on the elegant sofa with his arms in a 'T' and his legs splayed: king of the jungle. His belly spills forward, his expensive suit is tight across the chest.

she tells me the worst:
she doesn't know who she is any more

MAN FOUND DEAD IN CHILDREN'S PLAYGROUND

She screams as if she's on fire. We've heard it before, she's a *problem teenager*, Social Services *can't do anything with her.* We ignore her as we might ignore a fly dying on the window-sill.

depression sifts over me like a fine dust of skin

I didn't know that this dull-green spiky bush would let out such a profusion of pale yellow butterfly flowers

At Henry Street two police cars are parked in the road, and a woman is raising her voice behind the hedge. Around the corner someone has scattered breadcrumbs for the pigeons.

after lining up numbers into rows all morning I take a book of poetry into the garden

Three birds wheel in the sky, attached by an invisible string. When they reach the edges of their parabolas they slip into slow motion, and I wonder for a second if they might be kites or model aeroplanes. They circle and loop in the wind.

through raindrops: lupins, alliums, cordifolias, lilies

Sunset with boats:
the sky starts a slow pink
burns brighter and brighter
is red-orange as the sun slips out of sight

(flying fish)
the squat black silhouettes explode from the water, trace an arc and go back underneath with a - plosh -

in Lime House garden his Birds of Paradise plant has been conjuring these alien tangerine blooms for ten summers

(leeks in butter)
the smell of being-cooked-for like fingers pressed in deep between my shoulder-blades

A carpet of tiny proliferating flowers - squint and the whole corner of this paddock is a haze of purple-tinged blue. Vetch? Mum would know the right word.

Onion-brothers, their big purple pom-pom heads balance on their long straight stems, bobbing in the breeze like buoys.

old apple - it's sweet enough, but the texture reminds me of death

Another cat dead on the road. Outside the garage on the gravel, a cat-caught bird's underside teems with hungry life. Business as usual.

The sun is promising warmth. It gets people out into their gardens and then turns its back on them.

I pull a forgotten stone from the depths of my parka pocket - a beach weekend is attached to it like a veil.

june

by the roadside: new poppies like drops of blood on a mirror

the clock inside my stomach is running too fast - I'm losing time

The surface of the water is flat and dark, with a beard of frothy scum where the river-bed drops. I sit between bird shit and an empty rizla packet, trying not to look at the puddle of sputum on the pavement. The reflections of red brick buildings shimmer, hold their places.

a four-fingered scoop of shower gel; the colour, texture and zingy scent of the squidge from lemon meringue pie

(pavement treasures)
butter-yellow petals like shards of burst balloon / the back of a crisp packet - a midnight-blue mirror dotted with raindrops / my feet, splashing through the puddles

dog daisies on the roundabout: standing room only

The lady is so pleased to be asked how she is by the cashier (someone, anyone) that she tells her about her husband in the hospital, who has Alzheimer's. It is *a kind of bereavement, but not*.

(watching rain from the porch with the door open)
feather-soft sounds, a fresh green smell, the cold brush of air on my cheeks

Fatty's exhausted himself truffling about in the hedge all morning, eager for the scent of vole or fieldmouse. Yesterday he carried one whole in his mouth, only the tail drooping from one side. Now he lets go of his body, laying it across the rug like a corpse on a slab.

the yoga-class *ohms* slip under the door from a room down the corridor: a distant repeating fog-horn, a mammoth snoring, the twice distilled sound of calm

The morning mist is exactly the same blanched-almond colour as the sky. The tree-tops on the horizon are floating, set adrift from their roots.

rock rose petals: tissue-thin and crumpled like rejected love poems

A rectangle of wrapping paper, pinned up with a cherry-red pin. On it float twenty six small Japanese girls in red, orange and pink kimonos. Gold highlights glint when you tilt the paper. Their eyes smile.

I wasn't paying attention when I pegged out the clothes, but now it looks like someone spent hours deciding what should go where: chocolate brown, jade green, navy blue, jade green, aquamarine, pale green, chocolate

A fountain of branch-arms, each is feathered with elegant oval leaves and tipped with a clutch of bright orange blossoms, perfectly spherical, the size of boiled sweets. Close up their hundreds of flowers are concertina-ed paper, miniature Christmas decorations. The bees find them delicious.

Rain gets inside this fragrant coriander, this sinewy rosemary, prepares these tomato plants for letting out fat red pockets of juice.

Lucky dip:
A plump rosy radish with three mouthfuls of crunch, or a faintly blushing root with a swollen kink.

Silver lies belly-up, smiling. A curled paw shields her closed eyes from the too-bright light.

Sherfield Summer fete - who will win 'the dog with the waggiest tail'?

papery pink pea-blossoms hover over the green of the field
like stopped butterflies

fat breakfast blueberries let go of their stalks willingly,
nestle in my cupped hand like chicks

The sweet vegetable smell of grass hovers here all day, hanging around like heat from sunburnt skin. It waits for faces to dip down low and sniff it.

working outside on a sunny day:
even out here, my friend's emails can find me

easing the roots of forty new plants into the earth
is tucking forty children into bed

The tomato plants have gone thirsty all long hot day. They gift a cloud of their scent into the air - musky, full-bodied, sweet.

the red of poppies a gorgeous scum
risen to the surface of a field of wheat

Across a lilac-painted wall the sun has cast the shadows of pot plants - a zamioculcus, and something green and leafy with no label. The leaf motif is repeated, overlaid, in carefully-cut-out layers of grey tissue paper. A van passes and wipes the pattern clean.

Perfect sunshine. Emerging from a shade-dappled avenue of trees, the landscape opens up into fields of green wheat and grass. I catch a glimpse of a strip of pale purple, pull off the road to have a better look. This is where they grow the violet sweets they wrap in twists of plastic.

click off the noisy radio: hear a song written for two thrushes and the wind

while looking for something else, I find these words:
bloom where you are planted

july

Lie on your back on the grass, become quiet. One by one, they step forward. The chopped circle of the moon. Honeysuckle scent edging the breeze. Swallows weaving counterpoint, and above them an aeroplane in poor imitation. And next door's roses, punching holes into the evening, as red as the reddest lipstick.

The scraped-off layer bunches up like cobwebs, the latex glue-skin you peel off your fingertips. Underneath is smoother, a deepening rose. Later, colours will bloom around my knees.

such a loud song, once I've spotted his small brown shape he lets out another burst to convince me it's him

Last night there was yowling in the spaces between dreams. This morning there are opaque circles of crimson on the tiles near the cat-flap, where Fatty watched his nemesis through the scratched plastic and dripped from a hole in his neck. His fur is matted - when cut with nail scissors it releases a cloud of dark dust.

This morning we have killed a blackbird, a rabbit, a hedgehog and a deer with our hurrying machines. The small animal inside me quakes and grieves.

the garbage truck leaks a stink that curdles the air

'I love Milton Keynes' is sprayed in orange on the green bridge. Nearby a man sleeps on a bench through the sunny morning, an empty bottle of superstrong cider beside him. The bottle is the deep blue of late evening. The man's knees are drawn up towards his chest.

A muscle underneath the lower lashes of my right eye has mutinied. It vibrates in the mirror: the wings of a bird trapped in the corner of a room.

(what goes on in houses)
a beautiful thirteen year old girl with braided hair and luminous dark brown skin pushes away from her house on her bike, blinking a tear that splashes onto her top

long after rain, a patch of puddle in the car park holds a scrap of sky

Pushing water behind me
my muscles (who didn't
know they were tight) let go.
And let go. And let go.

Today there will be a break from our usual programming. Travel back through your day. Insert your own small stone >here<.

I want to describe the exact aroma of coffee, and sniff at the lip of the cup until I sneeze

Yesterday I waded through shin-high water in my living room. Today I eat aubergine wrapped around mozzarella in a hotel restaurant. Tomorrow we start mopping sewage from the kitchen floor. No problem.

(temporary home)
the cats pace the new rooms like men waiting to become fathers

after thirst, big gulps of icy lemonade

without squeaky shoes my bare feet make no noise on the grass, are happy soles

the fur stroked out
of her silver coat
rests on her back
downy dandelion seeds
waiting to be blown away
on a -puff- of breeze
to take root in
the earth, to grow

no time for being today - too busy doing

grain mustard
hook for drying cloth
olive oil
washing up liq
cat bisc + meat
butter
nuts to snack on
garlic

I open the curtains to a squirrel garlanding the tree in next door's garden. A pigeon sits patiently on a chimney stack. Behind, three blackbird dots rise up towards the ceiling of the sky.

the wind shaking the grass is more insistent than the rushing roar of metal on tarmac

The gravestone lists six children, all born to the same parents, all dead by thirteen. Study the dates (these two within three days of each other, this one four years later) and try to imagine the grief.

halo:
the music of raindrops on plastic

The ends of my hair are splitting.
They remind me I'm wearing out.

He doesn't like cats because they never do what you tell them to do. I like cats because they never do what you tell them to do.

a long journey, and at the other end - two otters plunging and rising up from the lake / apple and ginger tea, as good cold as it is hot / people I love

tic tac gone - enjoy the echo of mint on your tongue

After listening to Galway Kinnell we drive home through an avenue of trees. Thick golden light drips through the spaces between leaves. We are well-fed and drowsy. The air in the car is heavy with poetry.

today I saved the life of a pocket-sized mouse -
he had twitching whiskers and trembled in my hand

reading on a bench, the world opens up:
so much grass, so much sky

august

the sky half-lit, the day gravid with thousands of tiny births and tiny deaths

blackbird silhouettes rest on telegraph wires, move in shifting groups across the sky

He said he'd stop when his watch stopped, and he did.
When she gets to this part of the interview, her voice breaks.

Sixty inch-long caterpillars clot around the tender nettle tips. Every second or so they jerk their jet-black furry bodies in unison.

He answers the nurse's questions behind the hospital curtain. He’s John, lives in a hostel, doesn't have a partner. He has a brother but doesn't want him to see him like this. He doesn’t know his number anyway. His body is trying to get rid of something he's put inside it. He's been here before.

a sprinkling of cherries on the path beside the graveyard, most of them trodden to pulp

the pittering pattering rain accepts everything: dirty tissues, tarmac, brambles, skin a single nodding cyclamen in deep shade - tethered by its stalk - washed out flamingo pink against pale stone

The clean blue of the sky meets the striped blues of the water, where seagulls float like white corks. A woman in a navy blue sun-hat and a cherry swimsuit wades out towards the sail boats. The sea sings.

A coffee-cream bag covered in pink daisies and filled to the brim with apples: small, sunlit, smelling of lemons.

aquamarine mixed with plenty of white, flaking away from a battered garage door / a new front door circled by roses in matching sunshine yellow

His show-off tail feathers have fallen out but his neck is still the colour of polished lapis lazuli. I release a grey-blue frosted berry into a low arc and onto the grass. He picks his way over to it and takes it into his yellow beak, swallows. He circles shyly, waiting for more. Has he ever tasted blueberries before?

The whole bush shudders, as if trying to get rid of a sour memory. The clouds hurry on, not wanting to get involved.

Two skinny wolves - dark navy blue, mottled as if made of paper-mâché. The first stands on the steep dome of a hilltop, the second on the first's back. Claws out. They arch their elegant backs, their mouths are full of teeth like needle-tips.

I save the greenfinch, who has a cut over his eye, and who quakes in the hedgerow for an hour before crawling away to die. Later a blue-tit is scattered across the lawn.

the fuchsia hedge weeps petals into a spreading deep-pink puddle on the pavement at first attempt the tines bounce off the plastic skin of the gorgeous orange yolk

at noon the clouds are rushing and bumping overhead like London commuters

corn: hundreds of plump pale yellow kernels swaddled in papery green

a languorous gaggle of geese waggle their bottoms and groom their wings with lovely orange beaks

Storm: all this noise. The yellow lichen on the roof is nonplussed.

There's something unidentifiable on the lawn. Flies flick in, flick out.

The graveyard is scattered with crushed beer cans, silver streamers, empty bottles - the dead have been partying all night.

A row of cow-parsley skeletons, standing much taller than a man. Low morning rays wash the brittle stalks in watery gold.

at the weir the black Labrador throws his excited body into the water to lunge after ducks

the dandelion's circle of narrow petals is a happy splash of yellow poster-paint

Gold lettering on a pink sheet, rigged up on a roundabout: *Cheer up Matthew, we love you.*

Ride-out, Isle of Wight:
Tangerine orange, racing green, mint, candy pink, they centipede across the island and leave behind their stink.

after 8 hrs of driving:
numb bums

the wind shirring the roadside reeds / forty baby pheasants phweeing from their cages / chorizo and sun smoked tomatoes fizzling in a pan

Esther's garden: Pots dripping with lobelia, geraniums, gazania. A cat rolling on the bright patio. The sudden kerfuffle of pigeons shaking out their wings. A dark rose hiding at the back of the hedge. Being told the name of that acid orange flower and having to ask again ten minutes later. Montbretia.

september

I have something to tell you:
while it was raining, the sun rose

The toaster painting the bread golden, a black cat washing on the window-seat and pausing to tilt his whiskers up into the sun. Coffee in the pot, a warm house, a day full of good work lying itself before me.

between emails the blue-tits gobble blackberries outside my window from the edge of a busy road each car carries a rush of sound like a shroud

someone has posted the innards of a kebab - thin strips of lettuce stick to the red lip below the slot

Last night a man jumped from a hospital window. Too late to offer him this morning's small stone.

a roadside blanket of scrubby dark green shrub –
quietly nestled amongst the tired leaves,
a tiny five-petalled flower as white as paper

Sky bites: not pieces of sky, cool-blue and smooth in your palm, but oddments of pretzel nuggets covered in sesame, raisins, moss-green pumpkin seeds, sealed in plastic and handed out at thirty thousand feet.

(white)
a sharp ribbon of aeroplane exhaust, extending towards the horizon / mounds of early mist mistaken at first for pale-twigged shrubs / a plastic bag hunched on the verge imitating roadkill

asparagus fern - I'd like to bury my face in its frothy fronds

A felt-tip rainbow - orange, green, blue, red, yellow, orange. A shooting star with a short skirt. A red and yellow diagonally-striped sun with bad-hair-day rays. Tucked away in the corner, a squashed earth: green islands floating in the colour of late evening.

In a field near Darrow a sheep lies with her stomach wool pressed against the wet grass. On her back a crow shuffles a few paces forwards, settles, watches the morning come on.

3rd prize at the Sherfield Show in the 'animals made from fruit and vegetables' category - Erin's mouse - pear body, chili tail, fragments of avocado skin eyes, carrot stick feet and orange peel whiskers.

The mesenbryanthemum sat deformed and fat in its pot for months, the leaves growing low and plump as if filled with gas. The flowers started last week, a thrilling shock, fuck-off pink.

as she picked up the cellophane packet of 'unwashed rocket' that had fallen from her supermarket trolley, hot shame flushed through her

as I mix in dark muscavado sugar the plums squelch between my fingers

Blodges on the pavement: baked pink chewing gum, orangey butts folded over onto themselves, crumpled and glinting silver paper. They refuse to be beautiful, insist on something else.

he crouches near the edge of the river, throws gobs of torn-off bread for the greasy swans

walking home through the graveyard, the cold nips at my ankles

the last of the tomatoes:
as red and as sweet as the first

The planks lift and creak as two ladies sink their bottoms onto the bench. *Ah... it's a long way down, and a long way back up again.* They sit and watch the butterflies kissing the purpley-blue verbena. The summer is nearly finished. One of them lets out a word like blowing a perfect smoke-ring: *bliss.*

An ordinary looking middle-aged black woman, she walks along the pavement shouting *I am a chicken! Let me lay my eggs!*' She flaps her madness around her like Joseph's coat.

In the funeral parlour window a square white granite vase, big enough for only three letters: MUM

His 18 year old inked-in skin is still raised in weals,
it'll live with him for all the years he has left.

the street light tastes the dark – pring! –
time to brighten the street

black earl grey breathes out the scent of white flowers

the Dutchman's voice chases us around the quiet gardens

It's as if crushed rose petals stirred into milk were spilt across her cheeks. The rest of her skin pale. Her hair dark. Her eyes. Does she know how beautiful she is?

How to plant bulbs:
Spend a long time flicking through the catalogues: can-can girls, bright spurts, flouncy flirts, serious dark tulips. Plant the bulbs in clutches. Splash purple around the bird feeder, ring trees in yellow, dot red against white walls. Enjoy pushing the plump promises into the earth. Become a squirrel. Forget where you've planted them, forget that you've planted them at all. Get on with your life.

Quarter to nine:
I look and look at the huge full moon

october

a crown-shaped tree crowded with golden leaves
basking in the golden autumn light

early morning - an apple sits quietly intact in the middle of the road

roast red Rooster potatoes: dark pink curls of skin clothe the wooden chopping board

I shine the conker with my thumb all morning but the genie stays inside

after slotting fifty fritillary bulbs into the close dark earth I leave a trail of wet cut grass in four different rooms before I look over my shoulder

John the lawn-mowing-man's overalls are held up over his Santa-belly with string.

Deep in the tangled centre of the rosemary bush, a drop of water is holding on to the tip of a leaf. Its circle of brilliant light pokes you in the eye. Turn your head a fraction and it's gone.

Against a background of shifting pampas grass shadows,
a single yellow leaf sashays down onto the gravel.

(weather)
outside: cold and grey
inside: changeable

He wrote this poem when he was 18. That desolate part of him aches and keens.

This morning the sun has chosen to spotlight a clump of dead weeds, grown through cracks in the concrete. Their spiked heads twitch in the breeze - confused metronomes, annoyed cat's tails. They are the pale honey colour of a girl's hair.

A speeding ambulance glides past, blue lights flashing.
A woman opens her mouth, no sound comes out.

I can't tell you how red these leaves are…

He crosses the road - mid thirties, greasy blond hair, a huge black puffa jacket. When he gets to the corner he stops dead and stands motionless with a blank face as if he's trying to keep his balance. He stands and stands.

The lights buzzing, the PCs humming, the tippety tap and click click click of the office choir on a lonely Tuesday morning.

The builder high up on the scaffolding opens his arms and sings. I catch his mate's eye, we exchange a look.

wisps of spiderweb light drift past

Where the red pencil's body meets his neck, his red costume has been shaved into a ring of curves like a frilly collar.

the longer I stare at the screen, the more my brain fidgets in its skull

the ghostly face of a pansy leaves a smear of yellow on the dark

the sound of rain sets off a thousand tiny blossomings

only a few ochre leaves left flapping on the tree, not clinging on but resting their flat bodies on the air a mouthful of blue smoke leaks from the halfway-wound-down window and sits in the air before letting go of itself

A freshly ploughed field baked until delicious - clods of earth sit on the surface like crumbs.

mushrooming clouds of sweet-rot aroma plume from the stuttering strimmer the headlights swing into the drive and a hedgehog runs in all the wrong directions, finally disappearing into the dark corners of the evening

tiny Goldcrest with a streak of pollen-gold across his crown, he peeps a note so high you have to stand on your tip-toes to hear it

gulls trawl behind the tractor, gobbling up the fresh pink worms the blades have pulled from the earth

(bramble)
two raggedy blossoms, torn pink scraps, remain amongst the shrivelled fruit

this daffodil has already sent a blunt green periscope up above the earth

the days fall into the past like autumn leaves

november

early morning: the first hints of blue, and the lights in the far distance become ships floating miles above the sea floor, cold water slapping against their sides

white-breath morning: frost-brittle leaves make a hollow scratching sound as they touch down

On the verge where the trees bend low a dead bouquet leans against a wooden cross. Has her foot been caught at this spot? Does she watch deer nosing their way out of the woods at dawn? Does the whoosh of wheels break up long nights? Does she wait for new flowers?

no spaces in the hospital car park: cars circle like vultures

on the way home an argument explodes into the car as if an artery has been slashed

making fire inside on a November afternoon:
the smell of woodsmoke follows us to the car

the credit card rives the ice from the windscreen glass in clean crumbling sheets

peppermint tea:
clear green, a waft of pine needles

PREPARE FOR NERVE-SHREDDING TERROR!
says the bus

I watch eight seagulls lined up on the rail until a pigeon spoils their symmetry. The ducks and geese gathered around my shadow tread water. The cold pulls tears from my eyes.

A bowl of light, balanced on a pole, looks down on the shivering tree. The leaves are tired, ready to let go.

the metal bird's sketched downy lines of white
bleed out, soften, dissipate into blue

a glob of light wobbles as the blade of grass flickers in the breeze

In the Charity shop her steamer has just leaked water all over the floor. They *couldn't do without it*, it *brings the clothes up nice.*

The bush's branches are clotted with red berries. From inside the house three ginger cats eye me as I walk past.

Very-small-boy-in-a-bright-green-raincoat's father:
Now you're all wet, you chump. No more puddles for you.

lobster pink and scuffed with creamy cloud / bleak slate grey / the blue of deep water, jellyfish floating just out of view how has it taken me 33 years to notice a pigeon plunge his head into a murky puddle and gulp gulp gulp?

(Mushroom spotting)
Only two centimetres tall, a smooth dark chocolate pileus and a straight narrow stipe. Upside-down it - the chocolate hat's pulled under like a shower-cap and neatly rims the pure-white gills.

look up: families of white sparks are born and scatter, a handful of gravel flung on water

(Holiday)
The under-cover shopping mall was vast, the Haagen Dazs too creamy and too sweet. A hat and a pair of gloves each from the Pound shop kept them warm on walks along the beach.

a wasted journey gives me the time to think about something that might have remained unthunk

He's pushing his boy along an endless pavement between motorway and frosted grass. The two year old is crying hard. He stops and goes round to the front of the pram, tucking the boy's red face into his coat and stroking his hair. He whispers soft words; the child eats them like bread.

it isn't a bonfire in the distance, but a luminous orange wind-sock rippling in the wind

sitting in a cafe with sun streaming in
rearranging words until they fit

Fifteen minutes before the end of Sunday. I write this because I said I would. Rules hold me together.

a pile of spent matches on the hearth still hold the memory of heat and light

ten minutes of nothing, or rather ten minutes of paying attention to my breath, or rather ten minutes of returning my attention to my breath as my thoughts skip around like a five year old on Christmas morning

driving, late
fine rain blurs the night
spray blooms from the tarmac

a white rabbit bottom bobs in the beams before dissolving into the dark

december

bright morning:
two deer leap lightly across the frosted grass

A beetle on the keyboard with elegant ridges from his front to his back in bronze and cinnamon becomes what it is - a seed.

Rigg Bay
The dark seaweed is dusted with white and pops under our boots. Across the bay a family threads its way between the rocks, different sized dots racing back and forth between them and the edge of the sea. Dad counts twelve happy dogs through his binoculars.

The seagulls have gathered (hopefully) on the crest of the roof of the Loch Fyne Seafood Restaurant.

My palm is cobwebbed with wrinkles. When did they appear?

He's serving half-pints at The Cock in Auchenmalg, talking about the cows round and about. McKie's herd are 'crazy'. He comes out from behind the bar to properly demonstrate how they charge from the shed to their field, from their field back into the shed.

at the second hand car lot they're lined up in a long neat row, their headlights turned away from us, their boots all open as if they're lifting their skirts

He's leaning his big beefy arm out of the wound-down window, elbow bent. Crowds of cuddly toys cover the dashboard.

my fingers soften as the car fills with warm air

yesterday she stayed late at the office with a pair of sharp scissors, cut all the mouses free

A scooter cover, spattered with specks of white paint and flapping in the wind. Next door's black dustbin, mouth open and waiting to be fed. Bricks holding warmth inside. The dirty grey pavements ready to hold us up.

gulps of cold water: icicle-flavour

Disconsolate roses, their heads have become too heavy for their necks. They rest their blowsy pink chins on the edge of the glass.

half an avocado: with a thumb poked in, the skin comes willingly away from the slippery flesh

before the sun comes up
a cluster of bright pin-pricks transform a tree into a ship of light

A mass of rusty-red twigs, the hedge is a thrown-down endless length of mohair scarf. It warms the bare earth gap where the field-edges meet.

100 tiny fairy lights zig-zagging up the stairs
sprinkling light into the room like icing sugar

They have coated the paving stones by the river with ice - small girls in pink and silver glide in circles as their mothers make Christmas card lists in their heads.

a woman and her sniffly buggy-ed baby trail a cloud of eucalyptus scent - pale green, shot through with burning

His 96 year old father is on his own after his sister died last fortnight. His father's new neighbour is too noisy, screams at her children all night. There is a vibration in his throat - a panic, a concentrated sadness. He leaves his bag of Christmas presents behind him on the train.

She says something, I say something, she says something. Deep down, foundations shift.

We look at posters calling for a vote for women. She talks about being one of four women in her department of eighty, and how she worries about losing her looks as this, at least, is an advantage to her.

(city)
a black PVC Santa leering from a costume shop window / 'SERIAL ARSONIST MAY BE BACK' / a souped-up car pulling a luminous blue shadow beneath it / 'who dunnit' in black paint across the probation office door

a new bubble of blood takes shape whenever I slide away the cotton wool

The tall lamp rocks in the wind - only a few centimetres where the neck bends over like a snowdrop, but enough to loosen its base rooted in the earth, enough to release the tension from its metal.

a naked tree strung with apples

A thin crescent moon reclines, relaxing after a long night's watch. Bird silhouettes pass from left to right. Behind them a satellite burns brighter than the brightest star.

(wet landscape)
a clay-coloured leaf face down, disguised as a frog / the wind worrying the japonica / umbrellas walking their owners to work / the marbled grey sky moving lazily upwards

the weeping willow trails its branches on the frozen ground, leafless and thinking of Spring

her unborn baby lies between them as they talk, listening to its mother's voice and waiting to hear its name

blackbird on bare branches, his beak a chip of flame

Fiona Robyn is a writer and blogger living in Hampshire with her partner, her cats Fatty and Silver, and her vegetable patch. Her previous books are 'Living Things', her first poetry collection, and 'A Year of Questions: How to slow down and fall in love with life'. Her website is at www.fionarobyn.com and *a small stone* continues at www.asmallstone.com.

www.ingramcontent.com/pod-product-compliance
Ingram Content Group UK Ltd.
Pitfield, Milton Keynes, MK11 3LW, UK
UKHW040602210726
13854UKWH00008B/1809

9 781409 204497